The Silent Struggle: Navigating Mental Health Challenges in the Workplace

Frederique Bergeron

Copyright © 2024 Frederique Bergeron

All rights reserved.

ISBN: 9798340869135

CONTENTS

1 Understanding the Crisis in Canada — 4

2 Bridging the Gap: Employers and Healthcare — 10

3 The Hidden Crisis of Workplace Mental Health — 14

4 The Financial Trap of Disability Payments — 19

5 Employer Challenges and the Need for Systemic Change — 24

6 Proactive Solutions for Employers — 29

7 Case Studies and Real-World Examples — 34

8 Mental Health and Manager Burnout — 39

1 UNDERSTANDING THE CRISIS IN CANADA

The Rise of Mental Health Challenges in Canada

The mental health landscape in Canada has been undergoing a significant shift over the past decade, with increasing awareness of mental illness paired with a growing recognition of the challenges posed by untreated conditions. The Canadian Mental Health Association (CMHA) reports that over 20% of Canadians experience mental illness in any given year, meaning that one in five people across the country is dealing with conditions like anxiety, depression, PTSD, and other mental health disorders.[1] These statistics are even more alarming in the context of the workplace, where stress, burnout, and the toll of mental health issues are pushing individuals and organizations to their breaking points.

In the modern Canadian workplace, the pace and complexity of work, combined with economic pressures, are intensifying mental health struggles. According to research conducted by the Centre for Addiction and Mental Health (CAMH), mental health conditions are now the leading cause of workplace disability in Canada, accounting for about 70% of disability costs.[2] The workplace environment—once viewed primarily through the lens of productivity, efficiency, and output—is increasingly being recognized as a significant contributor to, or mitigator of, employee well-being.

The COVID-19 pandemic, in particular, has played a pivotal role in exacerbating these challenges. Prior to the pandemic, stress, anxiety, and burnout were already major issues in the workplace, but post-pandemic, these conditions have surged. The ongoing debates and uncertainty around remote work, along with blurred work-life boundaries, isolation, and future unpredictability, have added layers of complexity to the mental health challenges employees face. Mental health hotlines, including those operated by the CMHA, saw a significant increase in calls during and after the pandemic, many of them from employees seeking help for new or worsened mental health issues tied to workplace demands.

Prevalence of Mental Health Disorders

The statistics are sobering: depression, anxiety, PTSD, and burnout are now commonplace in Canadian workplaces, particularly in industries where emotional and psychological demands are higher. According to the Mental

Health Commission of Canada, depression and anxiety disorders alone account for more than 30% of disability claims.[3] Among those who have experienced burnout, 80% report a negative impact on their work, with significant losses in productivity, motivation, and job satisfaction.[4]

In addition to depression and anxiety, post-traumatic stress disorder (PTSD) is becoming more prevalent, especially in sectors like healthcare, first responders, and the military. The Canadian military and emergency services have recognized the importance of addressing PTSD within their ranks, but the disorder is often underreported in other sectors. Burnout, a condition characterized by emotional exhaustion, detachment, and reduced performance, has also risen sharply, particularly in "helping" professions such as social work, healthcare, and education.

The pandemic added further strain, particularly for those in essential services. Healthcare workers, already operating under intense stress, found themselves overwhelmed during COVID-19, leading to spikes in PTSD, anxiety, and burnout. During the pandemic, nearly half of Canadian nurses experienced significant mental health challenges, according to reports from industry sources. Teachers, too, faced unprecedented stress as they navigated online teaching, lack of resources, and heightened expectations, contributing to increasing mental health claims within the education sector.

The Economic Impact

Mental health issues in the workplace carry an enormous financial cost for Canadian businesses. Each year, untreated mental health conditions cost the Canadian economy over $50 billion, with a large portion of that figure attributed to workplace-related issues.[5] The costs of absenteeism (when employees take time off due to mental health conditions), presenteeism (when employees show up to work but are unable to function productively), and direct healthcare expenses all contribute to this staggering figure.

Absenteeism due to mental health conditions has seen a sharp rise, with estimates showing that one in four disability claims in Canada are related to mental health. Employees with untreated conditions such as depression or anxiety may miss work frequently, further compounding the financial burden on businesses. However, the more hidden cost is presenteeism, where employees come to work but are unable to fully engage or perform their duties. Presenteeism, which affects daily productivity, is estimated to cost significantly more than absenteeism, with some estimates suggesting it could be as much as 7.5 times higher.

Direct healthcare costs also weigh heavily on the economy. Businesses and insurance companies spend billions annually on mental health treatment, disability claims, and extended leave programs. Moreover, businesses without comprehensive mental health support systems often experience higher turnover rates, leading to additional recruitment and training expenses. The long-term costs of ignoring mental health are substantial, and businesses are slowly realizing that investing in mental health initiatives is not just a matter of employee well-being but also a sound financial decision.

Industry-Specific Vulnerabilities

Mental health issues do not affect all industries equally. In certain sectors, the prevalence of mental health conditions like burnout, depression, and anxiety is significantly higher due to the nature of the work. Healthcare, education, social services, and law enforcement are among the industries hardest hit by mental health challenges. These sectors involve high emotional labour, intense pressure, and an overwhelming sense of responsibility for the well-being of others, all of which contribute to elevated levels of stress and burnout.

In healthcare, for example, the emotional toll of caring for patients, especially during critical moments like the COVID-19 pandemic, has led to an epidemic of mental health issues. Nurses and doctors face a constant stream of life-and-death decisions, which can result in chronic stress, anxiety, and PTSD. In a study by the Canadian Medical Association, almost half of all physicians surveyed reported feeling burned out, and nearly 48% admitted to experiencing depression.[6]

Similarly, teachers in Canada are increasingly reporting high levels of stress and burnout, often due to increasing workloads, lack of resources, and the pressure of managing both in-person and virtual classrooms. A survey conducted by the Canadian Teachers' Federation found that nearly 70% of teachers described their stress levels as "high" or "very high," with many citing mental health issues as a primary concern.[7]

Other sectors, such as tech and finance, also face mental health challenges, though the pressures in these industries are different. In tech, for instance, long hours, tight deadlines, and the pressure to innovate can lead to chronic stress and burnout. Similarly, finance professionals often work in high-stakes environments where job security is uncertain, and the expectation to perform under pressure is immense. Both industries, while less focused on emotional labour, experience high rates of anxiety and burnout due to these work pressures.

The Stigma of Mental Health in the Workplace

Despite growing awareness of mental health issues, stigma continues to be a significant barrier for employees seeking help. In many Canadian workplaces, there is a lingering belief that mental health struggles are a sign of weakness, which can lead to career stagnation or even job loss. This stigma discourages employees from disclosing their mental health conditions or seeking the accommodations they need to recover and function at their best.

According to a survey conducted by Morneau Shepell, 78% of employees in Canada believe that disclosing a mental health issue would negatively impact their career prospects, such as being passed over for promotions or excluded from important projects.[8] This fear is not unfounded; stigma in the workplace can manifest subtly through exclusion, lack of support, or downplaying of mental health struggles. In some industries, particularly those that are male-dominated or have a "tough" culture, such as construction or law enforcement, there is a prevailing attitude that mental health problems are a personal issue to be dealt with privately, rather than an issue that deserves attention and accommodation.

How Stigma Manifests

Stigma doesn't always look like overt discrimination or exclusion. In many cases, it can be more insidious. Employees who disclose mental health conditions might find themselves being subtly excluded from key projects or opportunities, their abilities and commitment called into question. In environments that prize toughness or endurance, such as finance or law, admitting to a mental health struggle can be seen as a career-ending move. For example, a lawyer who admits to struggling with depression might be perceived as unreliable, leading to fewer client-facing responsibilities or being passed over for partnership.

Stigma also manifests in the way personal struggles are often dismissed or minimized. In many workplaces, employees may hear phrases like "Just tough it out" or "Everyone gets stressed, it's part of the job," which trivialize their experiences and discourage them from seeking help. These attitudes create an environment where mental health is not taken seriously, leading employees to hide their struggles until they become overwhelming.

The Impact of Stigma on Seeking Help

The fear of stigma can prevent employees from accessing the resources and accommodations they need. Studies have shown that employees who feel stigmatized are less likely to seek help, leading to a cycle of untreated mental health issues that grow worse over time. Employees who fear being judged or perceived as weak often push through in silence, only to reach a breaking point where they can no longer function effectively at work.

This reluctance to seek help contributes to the larger mental health crisis in Canada. Untreated conditions lead to increased absenteeism, presenteeism, and, ultimately, longer-term disability leaves. For employers, the failure to address mental health issues early on can result in higher costs down the road, as untreated conditions escalate into more severe, chronic problems that require extended absences or even permanent disability.

Shifting the Narrative

Despite these challenges, some Canadian businesses are beginning to lead the way in reducing stigma and promoting mental health in the workplace. Initiatives like Bell's Let's Talk campaign have helped normalize conversations about mental health and reduce the stigma associated with seeking help. By creating an open dialogue, these initiatives encourage employees to address mental health issues early, before they become debilitating.

Cultural change initiatives, such as mental health training for managers, peer support programs, and access to Employee Assistance Programs (EAPs), are also critical in shifting the narrative. Companies that invest in these programs demonstrate a commitment to employee well-being, which helps reduce the fear of seeking help and fosters a more supportive, stigma-free workplace environment.

While mental health challenges in the workplace are significant, there are steps that Canadian businesses can take to reduce stigma, promote mental well-being, and address the growing crisis. By recognizing the importance of mental health and investing in proactive solutions, employers can create healthier, more productive work environments where employees feel supported and valued.

Endnotes

1. Canadian Mental Health Association. (2021). *Fast Facts about Mental Health and Mental Illness.* Fast Facts about Mental Health and Mental Illness - CMHA National
2. Centre for Addiction and Mental Health. (2020). *Workplace Mental Health A Review and Recommendations.* https://www.camh.ca/-/media/files/workplace-mental-health/workplacementalhealth-a-review-and-recommendations-pdf.pdf
3. Mental Health Commission of Canada. (2021). *Workplace Mental Health.* Workplace Mental Health - Mental Health Commission of Canada
4. Corporate Wellness Magazine. *The Science of Burnout: Understanding Its Causes, Symptoms, and Impact on Work Performance.* The Science of Burnout: Understanding Its Causes, Symptoms, and Impact on Work Performance | Corporate Wellness | Employee Well-Being (corporatewellnessmagazine.com)
5. Mental Health Commission of Canada. (2013) *Making the Case for Investing in Mental Health in Canada.* Making the Case for Investing in Mental Health in Canada - Mental Health Commission of Canada
6. Canadian Medical Association, (2021) *A profession under pressure: results from the CMA's 2021 National Physician Health Survey.* A profession under pressure: results from the CMA's 2021 National Physician Health Survey | CMA
7. Canadian Teachers Federation. (2021) *Teacher Mental Health Check-in Survey.* Doc-13-1-Pandemic-Research-Report-Teacher-Mental-Health-Check-in-Survey_updated.pdf (shopify.com)
8. Mental Health Commission of Canada. (2017) *Understanding mental health, mental illness, and their impacts in the workplace.* Monreau_White_Paper_Report_Eng.pdf (mentalhealthcommission.ca)

2 BRIDGING THE GAP: EMPLOYERS AND HEALTHCARE

The world of mental health care in Canada is a complicated landscape for those trying to navigate it, and nowhere is this more apparent than in the disconnect between the key stakeholders: employers, healthcare providers, and insurance companies. This misalignment creates a fragmented system where employees seeking support for mental health issues often find themselves caught in a web of confusion, delayed treatment, and inadequate support. While each party involved has its priorities—employers need productivity, healthcare providers focus on health, and insurance companies are concerned with costs—the lack of communication and cooperation among them leaves employees stranded without a clear path to recovery.

The Employer's Perspective

For employers, the need to balance compassion with productivity is not only challenging but often frustrating. When an employee presents a doctor's note stating that they require time off for "stress" or "anxiety," the vagueness of these diagnoses can leave employers unsure about how to proceed. Typically, these notes provide little detail beyond the recommendation for time off, lacking any mention of the employee's specific condition or what accommodations might facilitate a return to work.

Consider the case of Sarah, a manager at a mid-sized retail company in Toronto. When one of her top-performing employees, Emma, submitted a doctor's note citing stress and anxiety, Sarah was unsure how to handle the situation. The note offered no timeline for Emma's return, no insight into the nature of her condition, and no guidance on accommodations. Should Sarah lighten Emma's workload? Extend her time off indefinitely? Adjust her schedule to be more flexible when she does return? Without clear direction, Sarah was left to guess, all while worrying about the potential legal and ethical ramifications of mishandling the situation.

Employers in Canada are required by law to provide accommodations under the Canadian Human Rights Code and other relevant legislation, but this duty becomes murky when medical guidance is vague or lacking. In situations like Sarah's, employers may inadvertently either overaccommodate or underaccommodate, leading to prolonged absences or mismanaged returns to work. For Sarah, her attempts to manage Emma's absence led to other employees becoming overloaded, as they picked up Emma's responsibilities. This, in turn, caused resentment and burnout among her team, ultimately disrupting the entire department's productivity.

On the other side of this coin, some employers might feel trapped between wanting to support their employees and needing them to perform. For those in smaller businesses or industries where every position is critical, having an employee on an extended leave can cause a domino effect of delays and financial strain. The employer's frustration may grow when they are left with unclear information on whether the employee will return in a matter of weeks or months, or if they will be able to perform their previous role. The process is so opaque that many managers report feeling powerless, with no clear guidance or timelines to rely on.

Healthcare Providers' and Insurers' Roles

While employers grapple with how to accommodate employees, healthcare providers face their own challenges. Doctors and mental health professionals are focused on patient care, but they are often disconnected from the practical realities of workplace reintegration. For a healthcare provider, the priority is ensuring that the patient—whether suffering from anxiety, depression, PTSD, or another mental health condition—has the space and time to recover. As a result, they may recommend extended time off, which helps the patient in the short term but doesn't address the longer-term question of how they will eventually reintegrate into the workplace.

Doctors are often hesitant to provide detailed information in their notes due to concerns about patient confidentiality. While privacy laws are essential for protecting individuals, they inadvertently create challenges for employers who need enough information to make informed decisions about accommodations. For example, if a doctor provides a note that simply states "the employee is suffering from anxiety," it doesn't clarify the severity of the condition, the expected timeline for recovery, or what specific workplace stressors might have triggered the condition. This leaves the employer in the dark, trying to accommodate the employee without knowing what kind of accommodations are actually needed.

Moreover, healthcare providers may not always consider the realities of the workplace. Returning to work is often framed as an eventual goal, but without a detailed plan for that transition, the employee's return may be rocky. It's not uncommon for employees to come back prematurely or without the necessary supports, leading to relapses and further time off.

Take the case of David, a software engineer at a tech firm who was diagnosed with depression and given three months of medical leave. His doctor provided a note indicating the need for time off, but nothing more. When David felt ready to return, he was thrust back into a high-pressure environment without any changes to his workload or schedule. Within weeks, his condition worsened, and he had to take additional leave. Had there been more communication between David's healthcare provider and his employer, a phased return with lighter duties might have prevented this cycle.

Insurance companies further complicate the situation. Mental health conditions are often subjective in nature, making them harder to document than physical ailments. Insurance companies, driven by the need to manage costs, frequently require extensive and specific documentation to approve claims. This can create barriers for employees who may already be struggling emotionally and mentally. The need to submit multiple reports, medical assessments, and ongoing proof of treatment can deter employees from filing claims at all or delay access to much-needed financial support.

For example, let's look at Karen, a financial analyst who was diagnosed with PTSD after a traumatic car accident. Her initial short-term disability claim was denied because her insurance company demanded more detailed documentation about her therapy sessions and recovery progress. Her therapist, citing privacy concerns and time constraints, was unable to provide the level of detail requested. As a result, Karen was left without financial support for several months, causing additional stress that worsened her condition. The very system designed to support employees like Karen in times of need was actually creating more hurdles for her to navigate.

The Communication Breakdown

What's clear in all of these examples is the profound breakdown in communication between the key players. Employers, doctors, and insurers are often working in silos, each with their own objectives, and there is rarely a collaborative approach to ensuring the employee's well-being and return to work.

For instance, employers are left to guess what accommodations will be helpful because doctors rarely provide specific recommendations, and insurance companies may not approve claims without burdensome documentation. In this fractured system, employees find themselves juggling the pressures of recovering from a mental health issue while also trying to navigate bureaucratic processes that are neither streamlined nor sensitive to their needs.

This lack of coordination can lead to situations where an employee's return to work is either delayed or handled poorly. Employees may return without adequate preparation, only to leave again due to relapses, while employers struggle with how to provide the right support. Meanwhile, insurance companies continue to focus on limiting payouts rather than facilitating recovery.

Finding Solutions Through Better Communication

So how can this cycle of miscommunication be broken? The answer lies in fostering better communication protocols and collaboration between employers, healthcare providers, and insurers. One potential solution is the establishment of partnerships between employers and mental health professionals. For example, having a designated mental health liaison—a psychologist or counselor—who can act as an intermediary between the employer and the employee's healthcare team can provide valuable insight into the employee's condition while maintaining privacy. This liaison could offer guidance on accommodations, suggest timelines for reintegration, and help craft a phased return-to-work plan that works for both the employee and the employer.

Similarly, insurance companies need to reconsider their approach to mental health claims. By adopting a more compassionate, flexible approach that prioritizes recovery over rigid documentation requirements, insurers can help reduce the financial strain on employees and expedite their return to work. For instance, accepting telehealth sessions and virtual therapy as legitimate treatment options would make it easier for employees to access care and provide the necessary documentation. Reducing the burden of proof for mental health claims would also help employees get the support they need more quickly, preventing conditions from worsening.

Finally, the development of comprehensive mental health policies at the organizational level is key. These policies should include clear processes for requesting accommodations, steps for managers to follow when an employee is struggling with mental health, and guidelines for collaboration with healthcare providers. A proactive approach would include regular check-ins, access to Employee Assistance Programs (EAPs), and training for managers on how to support employees dealing with mental health challenges.

The current disparity between employers, healthcare providers, and insurance companies in Canada exacerbates the difficulties faced by employees with mental health conditions. Each stakeholder operates with limited visibility into the others' priorities, leaving employees caught in a system that often delays their recovery. By fostering better communication, streamlining processes, and creating collaborative approaches to mental health, the system can be transformed to support employees' well-being and facilitate smoother transitions back to work.

3 THE HIDDEN CRISIS OF WORKPLACE MENTAL HEALTH

The reality of untreated mental health issues in the workplace is a silent crisis, one that often goes unnoticed by managers, employers, and even coworkers until it's too late. Many employees show up to work every day with untreated mental health conditions, balancing the weight of their internal struggles while trying to maintain outward professionalism. While their presence might suggest they are functioning, the reality is far more complex. Untreated mental health issues lead to high absenteeism, presenteeism, breakdowns in communication, and a significant dip in productivity. These issues not only affect the individual but also ripple across teams, damaging workplace culture and business performance.

Employees Struggling Without Proper Diagnosis or Treatment

Employees suffering from mental health conditions often keep these struggles hidden, either out of fear of stigma or because they have not sought or received a proper diagnosis. Nearly 40% of Canadian workers have reported that workplace stress has contributed to their mental health struggles, though many hesitate to seek help. Despite growing awareness around mental health, several barriers prevent employees from addressing their mental health conditions.

Why Mental Health Goes Untreated

Stigma remains one of the most significant barriers to mental health treatment in the workplace. Although campaigns like Bell Let's Talk have helped reduce the stigma around mental health in Canada, many employees still fear that admitting they are struggling will negatively affect their careers. As noted in chapter one, a survey by Morneau Shepell revealed that 78% of employees believed that disclosing a mental health condition could lead to career stagnation or even job loss. These fears are not unfounded—many workers worry that they will be perceived as weak or less capable than their peers, which could affect opportunities for promotion or involvement in high-profile projects.

Cost is another significant barrier. While mental health services in Canada are covered to some extent by public healthcare systems, many essential treatments—such as therapy, counseling, and medication—require additional out-of-pocket expenses. For individuals who do not have comprehensive health insurance through their employers, these costs can be prohibitive. This financial burden leads many to avoid seeking the help they need, causing their conditions to worsen over time.

Fear of workplace repercussions is another factor. Employees may worry that taking time off to seek treatment will result in negative performance reviews or damage their relationships with managers. Many feel that their professional reputations are tied to their ability to persevere leading them to endure mental health challenges in silence rather than risk being seen as less competent. These unspoken fears contribute to the cycle of untreated mental health, as individuals keep pushing through until they reach a breaking point.

The Costs of Untreated Mental Health

Untreated mental health issues come at a significant cost, both for employees and employers. For employees, the personal toll is substantial—chronic anxiety, depression, or stress not only diminishes their quality of life but also affects their ability to focus, make decisions, and engage meaningfully at work. Over time, this lack of engagement can result in burnout, emotional exhaustion, and, ultimately, job loss.

For employers, the costs are more than just human—they are financial. A report from Deloitte Canada found that for every dollar invested in mental health initiatives, companies saw a return of $2.18 in reduced absenteeism and turnover.[1] Employees who struggle with untreated mental health conditions often take more sick days, leading to higher absenteeism. Even when they are present, these employees may not be fully engaged in their work, leading to a phenomenon known as presenteeism—when individuals are physically present but unable to perform effectively.

Presenteeism can be far more costly than absenteeism. Employees experiencing mental health issues may take longer to complete tasks, make more mistakes, or require more oversight from managers. These issues erode overall team performance and create inefficiencies in business operations. Over time, untreated mental health issues can lead to higher turnover, as employees who lack the necessary support may leave voluntarily or face performance-related termination

Case Study of a Silent Struggler

Let's consider the case of Claire, a project manager in a large advertising agency based in Toronto. Claire had always been known for her attention to detail and strong leadership skills, but after a series of personal challenges, she began to struggle with depression. At first, Claire kept her struggles to herself, fearing that disclosing her mental health condition would lead her superiors to question her ability to manage large accounts.

Claire's performance slowly began to decline. She missed deadlines, became more irritable with her team, and found it increasingly difficult to focus on her tasks. Her coworkers noticed the changes, but none of them felt comfortable addressing the issue directly. Claire, too, felt trapped—she didn't want to be seen as weak or incapable, so she pushed through her workday in a state of silent suffering.

Over time, Claire's condition worsened, and she began to take more and more sick days. Eventually, her manager, concerned about her productivity, placed her on a performance improvement plan. This only added to Claire's stress and anxiety, and within a few months, she resigned from her position. Had there been an earlier intervention—perhaps an open conversation with her manager or access to mental health resources—Claire might have received the support she needed and remained a valuable part of the team.

The Unprepared Employer

Unfortunately, many employers and managers lack the training and resources necessary to recognize when an employee is struggling with mental health issues, let alone how to offer support. In many workplaces, mental health is still treated as a taboo topic, or worse, a personal issue that employees should manage on their own time.

The Skills Gap

Most managers are trained to focus on performance metrics—sales numbers, project deadlines, and client satisfaction—but they are not taught how to identify signs of mental health distress in their teams. Many mental health issues manifest in subtle ways, such as withdrawal from team activities, mood swings, irritability, or missed deadlines. Without the proper training, managers may interpret these behaviours as poor performance or a lack of commitment, rather than recognizing them as potential warning signs of an underlying mental health condition.

For example, an employee who becomes increasingly withdrawn or irritable during team meetings may be struggling with anxiety or depression, but without the skills to recognize these signs, a manager might simply assume that the employee is disengaged or underperforming. Addressing mental health in the workplace requires more than just Human Resources policies—it requires active, ongoing training for managers and HR professionals to understand the complexities of mental health and how to offer meaningful support.

The Legal and Ethical Considerations

Employers also face legal and ethical challenges when managing employees with mental health conditions. In Canada, employers have a duty to accommodate employees with disabilities, including mental health conditions, under the Canadian Human Rights Act. However, navigating these accommodations without proper guidance can be challenging. Employers must strike a balance between respecting an employee's privacy and ensuring that appropriate accommodations are provided. Failure to provide accommodations can lead to human rights violations, while overstepping can result in legal repercussions.

For many employers, the fear of making a misstep leads to inaction. Without clear guidelines on how to support employees with mental health conditions, many managers avoid addressing the issue altogether, leaving employees to fend for themselves. This lack of action only worsens the situation, as untreated mental health issues grow more severe over time.

Providing Practical Resources

The solution lies in equipping employers with the tools and resources they need to support their teams effectively. Mental health first aid training, for example, has proven to be an effective tool for managers. This type of training teaches managers how to recognize early warning signs of mental health issues, how to offer support without crossing legal or ethical boundaries, and how to direct employees to the appropriate resources, such as Employee Assistance Programs (EAPs) or counseling services.

By investing in mental health training and creating a supportive workplace environment, employers can help reduce the stigma around mental health and encourage employees to seek help before their conditions worsen.

The Impact on Workplace Culture

When mental health struggles go untreated, the impact extends far beyond the individual. Team morale declines, communication breaks down, and workplace conflicts become more common. In environments where mental health is not addressed openly, employees who are struggling may feel isolated, while their coworkers become frustrated by the lack of support or understanding.

Examples of Culture Deterioration

In one company, an employee with undiagnosed bipolar disorder frequently missed deadlines, causing friction with their team. Coworkers, unaware of the underlying mental health issue, became resentful, as they had to pick up the slack. Over time, this resentment led to passive-aggressive behaviour, workplace conflicts, and a general decline in team morale. Without a proactive approach to addressing the employee's mental health, the entire team suffered, leading to high turnover rates and a toxic work environment.

Proactive Strategies to Protect Culture

To prevent these issues from escalating, companies must implement proactive strategies to protect workplace culture. Peer support networks enable employees to connect with coworkers who have faced similar challenges, fostering a sense of community and helping to alleviate feelings of isolation. Creating safe spaces for mental health discussions—whether through regular check-ins, wellness workshops, or mental health awareness campaigns—can also help reduce stigma and encourage employees to seek help.

Companies like WestJet and Bell have implemented mental health advocacy programs that focus on creating a culture of openness and support. These programs include access to counseling services, mental health training for managers, and regular wellness initiatives. By prioritizing mental health, these companies have seen significant improvements in employee engagement, productivity, and overall workplace satisfaction.

Untreated mental health in the workplace is a crisis that affects not only the individual employee but the entire organization. By recognizing the signs of mental health distress, providing proper support and training for managers, and fostering a culture of openness, employers can help reduce the personal and financial costs of untreated mental health conditions.

Endnotes

1. Deloitte. (2019). *Deloitte research reveals significant return on investment for workplace mental health programs.* Deloitte research reveals significant return on investment for workplace mental health programs | Deloitte Canada

4 THE FINANCIAL TRAP OF DISABILITY PAYMENTS

A Broken System

In Canada, the government's disability support system is meant to provide a financial safety net for individuals who are unable to work due to medical conditions. For those suffering from chronic mental health issues the ability to work consistently may be severely compromised. However, the current disability support framework—most notably, Canada Pension Plan (CPP) disability payments—fails to account for the unique challenges posed by mental health conditions.

While physical disabilities are easier to assess through medical tests or observable impairments, mental health conditions are often less visible and harder to quantify. This subjectivity, combined with the inadequate financial support provided by CPP and similar programs, leaves individuals with chronic mental health conditions in a precarious position. They are often trapped between the need to work and their inability to perform, unable to take the time necessary to heal due to financial insecurity.

The Financial Realities of Mental Health

The first harsh reality faced by those with chronic mental health issues is that the disability payments offered by government programs like CPP fall far short of their basic living expenses. According to Statistics Canada, the average CPP disability benefit in 2023 was approximately $1,053 per month. For those living in major cities like Vancouver or Toronto, where the cost of living is high, this amount barely covers rent, let alone groceries, utilities, or healthcare costs.

Lillian, a social worker from Vancouver, was diagnosed with severe depression. After months of struggling with her workload, her doctor recommended taking an extended leave. However, when Lillian applied for CPP disability benefits, she discovered the maximum monthly payout would barely cover half of her rent. With the threat of losing her apartment looming, she had no choice but to continue working, despite her rapidly deteriorating mental health.

Lillian's case is not unique. Many Canadians with mental health conditions are forced to remain in the workforce, even when they are not well enough to do so. This is especially true for those without supplemental disability insurance from their employers, which may provide a slightly higher monthly benefit than CPP but still falls short of covering the full cost of living. For employees like Lillian, the decision to keep working despite their condition is often one of survival rather than choice.

Barriers to Accessing Disability Payments

Even for those who are eligible for CPP disability benefits, accessing them is far from straightforward. Employees with mental health conditions frequently struggle to qualify for disability benefits due to the subjective nature of mental illness. Unlike physical injuries, which can be verified through diagnostic tests, mental health conditions rely on self-reporting, therapy notes, and sometimes the interpretation of healthcare providers.

Anxiety, depression, and PTSD can vary in severity from day to day, making it harder for individuals to "prove" that their condition is disabling. To qualify for CPP disability benefits, applicants must demonstrate that their condition is both "severe" and "prolonged," criteria that can be difficult to meet when dealing with fluctuating mental health symptoms.

Take the example of Daniel, an accountant in Montreal diagnosed with generalized anxiety disorder. While Daniel experienced extreme periods of panic and sleeplessness that prevented him from working effectively, his condition was not consistent. There were weeks when he felt capable of handling his work, only to be followed by episodes where he couldn't get out of bed. When Daniel applied for CPP disability benefits, his application was denied on the grounds that his condition was not considered "prolonged" enough to justify his inability to work full time. Despite his diagnosis, the cyclical nature of his condition worked against him in securing financial support.

Even when employees manage to qualify for benefits, the bureaucratic process is often long and draining, requiring extensive documentation from healthcare providers. For individuals already struggling with their mental health, the additional stress of navigating the application process can exacerbate their symptoms. Delays in approval often leave people in financial limbo, unable to afford necessary treatments or medications.

The Consequences of a Broken System

The consequences of this broken system are clear: individuals with chronic mental health issues are forced to continue working, despite being unable to function at full capacity. This not only worsens their mental health but also affects their performance at work, leading to absenteeism, frequent job changes, and financial instability.

Lillian, the social worker from Vancouver, experienced this firsthand. Unable to take time off to properly address her depression, she found herself making mistakes at work, which led to reprimands from her supervisor. Over time, the stress of underperforming only deepened her depression, creating a vicious cycle from which she could not escape. Eventually, Lillian was let go from her job. Without a source of income and with only minimal disability benefits to fall back on, she fell into financial hardship, unable to afford the therapy and medication she desperately needed.

This is a story repeated countless times across Canada, where individuals with mental health conditions find themselves slipping through the cracks of a system that was designed to protect them. For those living with mental health conditions, the financial trap becomes a cycle that is hard to break.

The Vicious Cycle

For many individuals, the financial reality of living with a chronic mental health condition means they cannot afford to take a break from work. But continuing to work while struggling with mental health issues often leads to poor performance, job loss, and financial instability—further exacerbating the condition that caused the issue in the first place.

Take Marie, for example, who worked in customer service for a large retail chain. Marie had been dealing with untreated anxiety for years, but with no other financial safety net, she felt she had no choice but to keep working. Her anxiety made it difficult for her to deal with customers, and her performance suffered. Eventually, after repeated absences and customer complaints, Marie was let go. With no steady income, her anxiety worsened, leading to panic attacks that made it impossible for her to look for new work. With the minimal disability payments she received, Marie struggled to pay her bills, creating an overwhelming sense of hopelessness.

Marie's experience demonstrates the financial and emotional toll of being trapped in a system that doesn't allow for the flexibility needed to accommodate mental health challenges. The Canadian disability system's rigidity leaves individuals like Marie caught between needing to work and being unable to perform at their jobs. This vicious cycle continues, with each job loss adding to their financial stress and further deteriorating their mental health.

The Lack of Flexibility in the System

One of the most glaring flaws in the Canadian disability system is its lack of flexibility. Individuals with chronic mental health conditions often experience fluctuations in their symptoms, meaning there are times when they may be able to work part-time or perform certain tasks, while other times they need full rest. However, the current system does not accommodate this kind of flexibility.

The criteria for receiving CPP disability benefits require individuals to prove that they are incapable of working at all. This all-or-nothing approach doesn't reflect the realities of mental health conditions, where individuals may have good days and bad days. A more flexible system that allows for part-time work or gradual reintegration into the workforce would better serve individuals with chronic conditions, enabling them to remain financially stable while managing their health.

No Safety Net

For individuals without family support or additional safety nets, the consequences of insufficient disability payments are even more dire. Many people in this situation have no one to rely on financially, and without sufficient disability benefits, they are left in precarious situations—struggling to afford basic necessities like rent, food, and medication.

Consider Raj, a factory worker in Ontario who developed severe PTSD after witnessing a traumatic workplace accident. Raj's condition made it impossible for him to continue working, but when he applied for disability benefits, he found that the payments were far too low to cover his family's expenses. With no family support to fall back on, Raj faced mounting debts and the risk of losing his home. His PTSD worsened as he struggled to keep his family afloat financially, creating a downward spiral that he found impossible to escape.

For those like Raj, the lack of a financial safety net means that mental health conditions worsen under the weight of financial pressure, leading to long-term consequences for both their health and their financial stability.

Proposed Policy Reforms

The current disability system in Canada is in urgent need of reform, especially when it comes to supporting individuals with mental health conditions. Several changes could help break the cycle of financial hardship and mental health deterioration:

Increase in Disability Payments: One of the most immediate needs is to increase the amount of disability payments for individuals living with chronic mental health conditions. Payments should reflect the true cost of living, particularly in high-cost urban areas, to ensure that individuals can afford basic necessities while taking the time to heal.

Reduced Barriers to Access: The process for qualifying for disability benefits needs to be streamlined. The subjective nature of mental health conditions should be taken into account, with a focus on the lived experience of the individual, rather than strict diagnostic criteria that are difficult to meet.

Flexibility in Work Options: Introducing more flexible work options for individuals with chronic mental health conditions could prevent many from falling into financial hardship. A system that allows for part-time work, or phased reintegration into the workforce, would enable individuals to maintain some level of income while managing their health.

Holistic Support Programs: Beyond financial support, individuals with mental health conditions need access to a broader range of services, including affordable therapy, counseling, and vocational rehabilitation programs that can help them transition back into the workforce when they are ready.

The current disability system in Canada leaves individuals with chronic mental health conditions trapped in a financial cycle that is difficult to escape. By increasing financial support, reducing barriers to accessing benefits, and introducing more flexible work options, policymakers can help break the vicious cycle and provide individuals with the support they need to recover and thrive.

5 EMPLOYER CHALLENGES AND THE NEED FOR SYSTEMIC CHANGE

When Employers Struggle to Offer Support

In Canada, the growing awareness around mental health has created a new challenge for employers: how to properly support their employees while managing the legal, financial, and operational realities of running a business. While many Canadian employers want to support their employees with mental health conditions, they often find themselves constrained by a lack of resources, inadequate communication from the healthcare system, and rigid requirements from the insurance industry. This leaves employers in a reactive position, trying to navigate a maze of unclear medical advice, liability concerns, and complicated regulations.

Employers are legally obligated to provide accommodations for employees with disabilities, including mental health conditions, under the Canadian Human Rights Code. However, mental health issues are often more complex and less visible than physical disabilities, making it difficult for employers to understand exactly what is required of them. Unlike a broken leg or a chronic physical condition, mental health issues can fluctuate and are not always accompanied by clear or quantifiable symptoms. As a result, employers often struggle to provide the right accommodations.

Challenges of Navigating the System

One of the primary challenges employers face when attempting to support an employee with a mental health condition is the lack of clear, actionable guidance from healthcare providers. Medical advice is often vague, with notes from doctors that simply recommend "time off for stress" or "reduced workload due to anxiety." These broad recommendations leave employers unsure of how to proceed—how much time off is needed? Should the workload be adjusted permanently, or is this a temporary accommodation? Without specific information, employers are left to make guesses, which can lead to either insufficient support or accommodations that do not meet the employee's needs.

Additionally, insurers further complicate the process by imposing rigid requirements for approving disability claims. Mental health conditions are often subjective and difficult to document, leading insurers to request extensive documentation that may be difficult for both employees and healthcare providers to supply. For example, an employee who lives with chronic depression may need several weeks or months off, but insurers may deny coverage if they feel the employee's documentation is insufficient. This leaves the employer in a bind—do they extend the time off and bear the cost themselves, or require the employee to return before they are ready?

Concerns about liability also make employers hesitant to act. Without clear guidance from insurers or healthcare providers, employers fear making mistakes that could lead to legal repercussions. For instance, if they do not provide the right accommodations, they risk facing human rights complaints. On the other hand, offering too many accommodations or keeping an employee on extended leave could result in financial strain on the company, especially for small businesses. This legal and financial tightrope often leaves employers feeling overwhelmed and unsure how to proceed.

The Costs of Inaction

When employers fail to address mental health issues in the workplace, the costs can be significant. Ignoring or inadequately addressing mental health challenges leads to higher turnover rates, increased absenteeism, and reduced productivity. As stated previously, a study by Deloitte found that businesses that invest in mental health programs see a return of $2.18 for every dollar spent, largely due to the reduction in absenteeism and turnover.

Take the case of a mid-sized manufacturing company that chose to ignore early signs of mental health issues among its employees. Workers began calling in sick more frequently, and the company saw a marked decline in productivity. Over time, several key employees left the organization, citing burnout and stress as reasons for their departure. The company had to hire and train new staff, which took months and cost tens of thousands of dollars. Had the company invested in a proactive mental health program or addressed the early signs of distress, it could have retained its employees and avoided these financial losses.

Moreover, when employees are not properly supported, they may become disengaged from their work, leading to presenteeism—a situation in which employees are physically present at work but unable to function at full capacity. Presenteeism is often more costly than absenteeism because the employee remains on payroll but is not contributing effectively to the company's goals. This can result in missed deadlines, poor customer service, and a general decline in workplace morale. The long-term costs of ignoring mental health are substantial, and businesses that do not address these issues early often pay the price in lost productivity, higher turnover, and damaged workplace culture.

What Needs to Change

To create a healthier and more productive workplace, systemic changes are needed. Employers must shift from a reactive approach to mental health—where they only address issues after they have escalated—to a proactive one, where mental health is embedded into the company's culture and operations. This shift requires better tools, clearer guidance from medical professionals, and more flexibility from insurance companies.

The Role of Collaboration

One of the most significant changes that needs to occur is greater collaboration between employers, healthcare providers, and insurers. The current system operates in silos, with each party working independently of the others, leading to miscommunication and delayed support for employees. Employers often feel disconnected from the healthcare system, receiving limited and vague information about how to accommodate their employees, while healthcare providers may not fully understand the workplace context in which their patients operate.

A potential solution lies in developing clearer communication channels between employers, doctors, and insurers. As outlined in previously, mental health professionals could act as liaisons between the healthcare system and the workplace, providing employers with specific, actionable guidance on how to support their employees without violating privacy laws. Insurers, too, need to adopt a more flexible approach to mental health claims, recognizing that mental health conditions do not fit neatly into the boxes used for physical injuries or illnesses. By streamlining documentation requirements and providing quicker approval for claims, insurers can help reduce the financial burden on both employers and employees.

Proposing Policy Reforms

To create a truly cohesive system, policy reforms are needed at both the governmental and organizational levels. Governments could introduce incentives for businesses that invest in mental health programs, such as tax breaks or subsidies for implementing Employee Assistance Programs (EAPs) and mental health training. Additionally, reforms to the medical documentation process would allow for clearer communication between healthcare providers and employers, ensuring that accommodations are tailored to the employee's needs while respecting their privacy.

For example, a standard framework for mental health-related accommodations could be developed, outlining specific actions that employers can take based on different conditions. This would provide businesses with the clarity they need to make informed decisions without fearing legal repercussions. Similarly, reforms that encourage insurers to cover more comprehensive mental health treatments—such as therapy or long-term counseling—would help reduce the financial strain on employees and prevent conditions from worsening due to lack of care.

Long-Term Mental Health Programs

While many companies focus on short-term solutions for mental health, such as offering time off or temporary workload adjustments, these measures do not address the root causes of mental health issues in the workplace. Canadian employers need to invest in long-term mental health programs that prioritize employee well-being throughout their careers, rather than simply reacting to crises as they arise.

Integrating Mental Health into Organizational Culture

To create lasting change, mental health must become an integral part of organizational culture. This means moving beyond isolated initiatives and embedding mental health into every aspect of the business—from leadership and management practices to day-to-day operations. When mental health is treated as a core component of workplace health, employees feel safer seeking help, knowing that their concerns will be taken seriously and addressed with empathy.

One way to integrate mental health into company culture is by providing regular training for both employees and managers. Managers, in particular, need to be equipped with the skills to recognize early warning signs of mental health issues and to approach conversations about mental health with sensitivity. By creating an environment where mental health is discussed openly and without stigma, businesses can encourage employees to seek help before their conditions worsen.

Companies can also implement proactive wellness programs that focus on prevention rather than cure. Offering stress management workshops, mindfulness training, and mental health awareness campaigns can help employees build resilience and reduce the likelihood of burnout. Peer support networks, where employees can connect with colleagues who have faced similar challenges, can also provide a valuable sense of community and support.

Examples of Successful Programs

Several Canadian companies have already integrated long-term mental health programs into their overall business strategies, demonstrating the benefits of this approach. TD Bank, for example, has made mental health a core part of its employee wellness program. The bank offers a wide range of mental health resources, including 24/7 access to counseling services, stress management workshops, and a peer support network. These programs have helped TD Bank reduce absenteeism, improve employee retention, and foster a more engaged and satisfied workforce.

As referenced in earlier chapters, Bell Canada is a great example of a company that has successfully implemented long-term mental health programs. Through its Bell Let's Talk initiative, the company has made mental health a central focus of its workplace culture. Bell provides employees with access to mental health resources, offers mental health training for managers, and hosts regular events to raise awareness about mental health in the workplace. These efforts have not only improved employee well-being but have also enhanced Bell's reputation as a company that values and supports its workforce.

While Canadian employers face significant challenges in addressing mental health in the workplace, systemic change is both necessary and possible. By fostering collaboration between employers, healthcare providers, and insurers, and by investing in long-term mental health programs that prioritize employee well-being, businesses can create healthier, more productive workplaces. The benefits of these changes are clear: reduced absenteeism, higher retention rates, and a more engaged, satisfied workforce.

6 PROACTIVE SOLUTIONS FOR EMPLOYERS

Mental health in the workplace has increasingly become a priority for employers. With the rising awareness of mental health issues and the profound impact they can have on employees' well-being and productivity, it is essential for businesses to take proactive steps in addressing these challenges. Waiting for problems to escalate can lead to employee burnout, increased absenteeism, and high turnover rates. To mitigate these risks, employers need to implement comprehensive, long-term strategies that support mental health. This chapter focuses on practical solutions, beginning with training and awareness, moving to policy development, and exploring the potential for collaboration between businesses and government.

Training and Awareness

One of the most effective ways to combat mental health issues in the workplace is through training and awareness. When leadership teams and employees are educated about mental health, they are better equipped to recognize early signs of distress and can take action before the situation worsens. This preventive approach is not only beneficial for the individual but also for the overall health of the organization.

Comprehensive Mental Health Training Programs

Training should not be seen as a one-time event. Ongoing education for managers, HR professionals, and staff helps build a workplace culture that truly supports mental health. A key component of this training is Mental Health First Aid (MHFA) programs. Similar to physical first aid, MHFA teaches individuals how to identify, understand, and respond to signs of mental health issues in their colleagues.

Several companies in Canada have successfully implemented MHFA programs with significant results. For instance, Bell Canada's Let's Talk campaign includes MHFA training as part of its larger mental health strategy. By training employees to recognize mental health challenges in themselves and others, the company has seen a reduction in stigma and an increase in employees seeking help early, preventing issues from becoming severe.

Another example is the Mental Health First Aid program implemented at the Bank of Montreal (BMO). BMO's program provides managers and employees with the tools they need to support their colleagues in a non-judgmental and effective way. This has been especially helpful in creating a supportive culture where employees feel comfortable discussing their mental health struggles without fear of repercussions.

The value of mental health training extends beyond crisis management. It promotes an environment where managers and staff can have open, empathetic conversations about mental health, reducing stigma and fostering a culture of acceptance and support.

Identifying the Early Warning Signs

Recognizing the early warning signs of mental health challenges is critical for intervention. Managers need to be equipped with practical tools to identify behavioural changes that may signal that an employee is struggling. Changes in behaviour, such as withdrawal from social interactions, frequent lateness, missed deadlines, or sudden drops in productivity, can be key indicators of underlying mental health issues.

Daily check-ins with employees and regular performance reviews provide managers with the opportunity to assess these signs and initiate supportive conversations. A simple checklist could include:

- Has the employee's behaviour changed drastically over the past few weeks?
- Is the employee disengaged in meetings or team activities?
- Are there frequent unexplained absences or requests for time off?
- Has the employee's performance dropped without a clear reason?

By integrating these assessments into regular manager-employee interactions, employers can identify concerns early and offer support before the situation escalates into a more significant mental health crisis.

Creating a Mental Health Literacy Culture

Training alone is not enough to change workplace culture; mental health literacy must become ingrained in the fabric of the organization. A company-wide culture where mental health is openly discussed helps prevent issues from escalating and encourages employees to seek help when needed. Regular workshops, webinars, and educational programs can help employees at all levels of the organization understand the importance of mental health and how they can contribute to a supportive environment.

For example, WestJet has made mental health literacy a core part of its employee engagement strategy. By hosting regular mental health workshops and wellness webinars, WestJet ensures that all employees are educated about mental health issues, understand the importance of self-care, and feel empowered to seek help when needed. This proactive approach has significantly improved workplace morale and reduced absenteeism rates within the company.

Employers can also encourage mental health discussions by creating safe spaces for these conversations. Offering peer support groups, promoting Employee Assistance Programs (EAPs), and organizing mental health awareness days are all effective strategies for fostering a culture of openness and support. When employees see that their organization takes mental health seriously and provides the resources to back it up, they are more likely to feel comfortable addressing their own mental health needs.

Mental Health Policies and Action Plans

While training and culture are essential, having clear and structured policies around mental health is crucial for long-term success. Policies provide a framework for how employers will handle mental health issues in the workplace and ensure that both employees and managers know their rights and responsibilities.

Best Practices for Creating Mental Health Policies

Mental health policies should go beyond the basic provisions required by law. Employers need to be proactive in offering wellness days, flexible schedules, and mental health leave as part of their benefits package. These policies send a clear message that the organization values mental well-being and is committed to supporting employees.

When drafting mental health policies, employers should consider:

Wellness Days: Allowing employees to take mental health days without needing to provide detailed explanations can help prevent burnout and reduce absenteeism in the long run.

Flexible Schedules: Mental health conditions often require flexibility. Offering employees the option to adjust their schedules can provide the space they need to manage their mental health effectively.

Mental Health Leave: Offering a formalized process for taking mental health leave, whether short-term or long-term, ensures that employees know they have the support they need without fearing job loss or career setbacks.

By clearly outlining these provisions in the employee handbook and during onboarding, employers can foster a workplace that prioritizes mental health and encourages employees to take the time they need to manage their well-being.

Structured Action Plans

Mental health issues in the workplace often requires a structured response. Action plans should clearly outline the steps that managers need to take when an employee experiences a mental health crisis. This might include:

- Immediate steps for ensuring the employee's safety.
- Contacting HR or the employee's designated support system.
- Offering accommodations or adjustments to their workload.
- Developing a support plan for the employee's recovery, including regular check-ins and access to mental health resources.

For instance, a large tech company in Canada developed a mental health crisis action plan that includes a 24-hour hotline for managers and employees to access immediate support. The plan also specifies the types of accommodations that can be offered, such as modified duties or temporary reassignment to a less stressful role. This structured approach ensures that managers are prepared and know how to respond appropriately, reducing the risk of mishandling mental health issues.

Return-to-Work Programs

For employees who take time off for mental health reasons, returning to work can be challenging. A well-structured return-to-work program helps ease this transition, ensuring that employees feel supported and are not overwhelmed as they reintegrate into the workplace.

Phased return-to-work programs, where employees gradually increase their workload over time, have proven to be effective. These programs should be tailored to the employee's needs and include regular check-ins with managers and Human Resources to assess their progress. Additionally, providing access to ongoing mental health support—such as therapy or counseling—can help prevent relapses and ensure that the employee's return is successful.

Government and Corporate Collaboration

Employers do not have to tackle mental health challenges on their own. By collaborating with the government and other external organizations, businesses can access a wealth of resources and support systems to enhance their mental health initiatives.

Leveraging Government Programs

Many Canadian businesses are unaware of the government programs available to help them implement mental health strategies. The National Standard of Canada for Psychological Health and Safety in the Workplace, for example, provides a comprehensive framework for promoting mental well-being in the workplace. This standard includes guidelines for identifying psychological risks, implementing preventive measures, and ensuring that employees have access to mental health resources.

Employers can use this framework to assess their current mental health policies and identify areas for improvement. By aligning with national standards, businesses can ensure that their mental health programs are not only effective but also compliant with best practices in the field.

Public-Private Partnerships for Mental Health

Collaboration between businesses and external mental health organizations can significantly improve workplace mental health support. For example, companies like TD Bank have partnered with mental health non-profits to provide access to external resources and expertise. These partnerships allow businesses to offer a broader range of services, such as specialized mental health counseling or resilience training for employees.

Government agencies also offer funding opportunities for businesses looking to enhance their mental health programs. By tapping into these resources, businesses can implement comprehensive mental health strategies without shouldering the full financial burden themselves.

Proactive solutions for mental health in the workplace require a multi-faceted approach. Through comprehensive training, clear policies, structured action plans, and collaboration with external organizations, employers can create a supportive environment that promotes mental well-being. By taking these proactive steps, businesses can reduce the stigma surrounding mental health, increase employee engagement, and improve overall productivity. The future of work depends on prioritizing mental health, and the time to act is now.

7 CASE STUDIES AND REAL-WORLD EXAMPLES

This chapter offers a deeper look into how Canadian companies across various industries have handled mental health challenges, showcasing both successes and failures. Through real-world case studies, we'll examine the practical implications of mental health support in the workplace and how different approaches have impacted employees and businesses alike. These examples demonstrate not only the challenges faced by organizations but also the opportunities for growth and positive change when mental health is made a priority.

Case Study 1: A Struggling Employee Without Proper Support

Meet Lisa, a 42-year-old administrative assistant based in Vancouver. Lisa had been living with undiagnosed anxiety and depression for years, managing her mental health challenges privately while juggling the demands of work and home life. She had worked at three different companies over a span of five years, but in each job, her mental health deteriorated further due to lack of support, unmanageable workloads, and financial pressures that forced her to stay employed despite her worsening condition.

At her first job, Lisa was a highly motivated employee, praised for her attention to detail and organizational skills. However, as her anxiety began to worsen, she struggled to keep up with her workload. Simple tasks like answering emails or completing reports became overwhelming. Lisa found herself procrastinating, feeling anxious, and making small errors she had never made before. Her colleagues noticed, but no one said anything.

Without any formal mental health training, her managers interpreted her behaviour as a sign of disengagement and lack of motivation. During her annual review, Lisa's performance was criticized. Her manager mentioned that she seemed "checked out" and "distracted," but there was no inquiry into what might be causing these changes. Feeling ashamed and unsupported, Lisa's anxiety worsened, leading her to take frequent sick days, which were unpaid because she had not disclosed a mental health issue. She knew that without a formal diagnosis, her employer would not provide any accommodations, and her fear of judgment kept her from seeking help.

When she finally left that job, Lisa took a position at another company, hoping for a fresh start. But her untreated anxiety and depression followed her. The financial pressure of supporting herself in one of the most expensive cities in Canada, combined with the stress of hiding her mental health struggles from her new employer, led to a severe burnout episode. Lisa found herself locked in a vicious cycle: she couldn't leave the workforce because she needed to pay her rent, but continuing to work in environments that didn't support her mental health only made her condition worse.

By the time Lisa reached her third job, she was emotionally exhausted. This company had no formal mental health policies, no access to mental health services, and a culture where discussing mental health was seen as unprofessional. Without any support or accommodations, Lisa continued to struggle, and her performance declined even further. Ultimately, Lisa was let go due to "performance issues," even though the underlying cause was her untreated mental health condition.

Analysis: The Financial and Emotional Toll

Lisa's experience is a painful reminder of the broken systems that exist in many workplaces. Despite being a dedicated employee, her mental health struggles were misunderstood and ignored, leading to job instability, financial strain, and emotional burnout. Lisa's inability to leave the workforce due to financial constraints exemplifies how the lack of proper mental health support in the workplace can push employees into deeper mental health crises.

The financial and emotional toll on Lisa was immense. She found herself in a cycle of starting new jobs, hoping things would improve, but ultimately facing the same challenges as her mental health deteriorated. Her inability to afford adequate mental health treatment, coupled with the lack of workplace support, left her feeling isolated and hopeless. Lisa's case highlights the urgent need for employers to adopt more proactive approaches to supporting mental health in the workplace, especially for employees who may be suffering in silence.

Case Study 2: A Company That Successfully Implemented Mental Health Training

In contrast to Lisa's experience, there are companies that have made mental health a priority and reaped the benefits of doing so. Take XYZ Technologies, a medium-sized tech company based in Toronto. Like many businesses in the tech sector, XYZ Technologies had a fast-paced, high-pressure work environment that led to frequent employee burnout. Over time, the company noticed a pattern: employees were taking more sick days, productivity was declining, and turnover rates were increasing.

The company's leadership team recognized that something needed to change. After conducting an internal survey, they discovered that mental health issues, including stress, anxiety, and burnout, were widespread across the organization. Many employees reported feeling overwhelmed by their workloads, but few felt comfortable discussing their struggles with their managers.

In response, XYZ Technologies decided to implement a comprehensive mental health training program for its management team. The training, delivered through a certified Mental Health First Aid (MHFA) provider, focused on teaching managers how to recognize the signs of mental health challenges, approach sensitive conversations with employees, and provide appropriate support. The training also covered how to create a more open and supportive workplace culture where mental health discussions were normalized and stigma was reduced.

The Results

The impact of the training was profound. Managers at XYZ Technologies began to notice early warning signs of mental health issues in their teams—changes in behaviour, dips in performance, or increased absences. Instead of waiting for the problems to escalate, they initiated conversations with employees, offering support and accommodations such as flexible work schedules or temporary workload adjustments.

The company also introduced regular mental health check-ins during team meetings, creating an environment where employees felt comfortable discussing their challenges. Over the course of a year, XYZ Technologies saw a significant reduction in absenteeism and a 15% improvement in employee retention. Employee engagement surveys showed higher satisfaction rates, and employees reported feeling more supported by their managers.

Analysis: A Proactive Approach that Worked

The success of XYZ Technologies demonstrates the power of mental health training and early intervention. By equipping managers with the tools and knowledge they needed to support their teams, the company was able to reduce burnout, increase productivity, and foster a more inclusive and supportive workplace culture. This case illustrates how mental health training can have a tangible impact on both employees and the organization as a whole.

Case Study 3: A Mental Health Partnership That Worked

Another example of effective mental health support comes from ABC Retail, a large Canadian retail company that recognized the growing mental health challenges faced by its workforce. Retail jobs are often high-stress, involving long hours, customer service demands, and unpredictable schedules. Over time, ABC Retail noticed an increase in mental health-related absences, and employees were reporting high levels of stress and burnout.

The company realized it needed to do more to support its employees, so it partnered with a local mental health organization to implement an Employee Assistance Program (EAP). The EAP provided employees with confidential access to professional mental health services, including counseling, therapy, and crisis intervention. Employees could access these services 24/7, either over the phone or in person, allowing them to seek help whenever they needed it.

In addition to the EAP, ABC Retail hosted monthly mental health awareness workshops, where employees could learn about stress management, resilience, and mindfulness techniques. These workshops were designed to build mental health literacy across the organization and empower employees to take control of their well-being.

The Impact of the Partnership

The results were significant. Within six months of launching the EAP, ABC Retail saw a 20% reduction in mental health-related absences. Employees reported feeling more supported by the company, and those who accessed the EAP services said they experienced improvements in their mental health and overall job satisfaction. The partnership with the mental health organization also helped the company create a more supportive culture, where employees felt comfortable discussing their mental health needs.

ABC Retail's proactive approach to mental health, coupled with its partnership with a local mental health organization, not only improved employee well-being but also strengthened the company's reputation as an employer that prioritizes mental health. This helped attract and retain top talent, further contributing to the company's success.

Analysis: The Power of Collaboration

The case of ABC Retail highlights the benefits of public-private partnerships in addressing workplace mental health. By leveraging the expertise of a mental health organization, ABC Retail was able to offer its employees comprehensive support that went beyond what the company could provide on its own. The EAP and mental health workshops empowered employees to take charge of their well-being, reducing absenteeism and improving overall workplace morale.

Lessons Learned and Practical Steps for Employers

These case studies offer valuable insights for employers looking to improve mental health support within their own organizations. The key takeaways include:
1. **Early Intervention is Crucial**: Employers must train managers to

recognize the early warning signs of mental health issues and take action before problems escalate.

2. **Fostering an Open Culture**: Creating an environment where mental health is openly discussed reduces stigma and encourages employees to seek help when needed.

3. **Providing Access to Mental Health Services**: Partnerships with mental health organizations and implementing EAPs can provide employees with the professional support they need.

4. **Offering Flexibility and Accommodations**: Flexible work schedules and accommodations can help employees manage their mental health while remaining productive.

By adopting these proactive strategies, employers can create healthier, more supportive workplaces that not only benefit employees but also improve overall business performance.

These real-world examples demonstrate the importance of taking a proactive approach to mental health in the workplace. Employers who invest in training, culture-building, and partnerships with mental health organizations are better equipped to support their employees and create a thriving, resilient workforce.

8 MENTAL HEALTH AND MANAGER BURNOUT

Mental health issues in the workplace are multifaceted and go beyond common understandings of recovery through rest, therapy, and accommodations. Some mental health conditions—particularly those involving long-term or recurring challenges—require ongoing support that can impact both individuals and their teams. This complexity creates significant challenges for managers and colleagues as they work to accommodate these needs while maintaining a healthy workplace environment.

Challenges in Supporting Chronic Mental Health

Workplace discussions about mental health often focus on conditions like anxiety or depression, which many believe can be resolved or improved with sufficient time off or appropriate treatment. However, for individuals managing chronic mental health conditions, such as personality disorders, this narrative oversimplifies the reality. Recovery may not follow a linear path, and these conditions can present ongoing challenges, both for the individual and the workplace.

Employees with conditions such as borderline personality disorder (BPD) or bipolar disorder may navigate fluctuating emotional states that affect their workplace interactions. These fluctuations can include emotional intensity, difficulties in regulating behaviour, or challenges in maintaining stable relationships at work. While treatment such as therapy and medication may help, these conditions often require ongoing management, and the symptoms can persist in ways that affect daily team dynamics.

It's important for managers to understand that these behaviours are not intentional or personal but are part of the individual's lived experience with their mental health condition. Recognizing this complexity helps build a more inclusive and empathetic approach to supporting the employee.

The Emotional Toll on Managers and Team Members

Supporting employees with chronic or complex mental health conditions can place significant emotional demands on managers and colleagues. Managers may find themselves balancing their responsibility to support the employee with the needs of the rest of the team. The emotional energy required to handle these situations—especially if they occur over long periods—can lead to emotional exhaustion and, in some cases, burnout.

For example, a manager who regularly assists an employee navigating mental health challenges might have to adjust schedules, mediate interpersonal conflicts, and offer emotional support while still meeting the demands of the job. Over time, this can lead to frustration and fatigue if the manager doesn't have the tools or resources to manage both their own well-being and that of the team.

Similarly, team members may experience emotional strain when they feel they are constantly adapting to the changing needs of a colleague. However, it's essential that these frustrations be handled with sensitivity, ensuring that the employee experiencing mental health challenges is not isolated or stigmatized. Fostering open communication and providing clear, compassionate pathways for addressing these challenges can prevent the buildup of tension within the team.

The Concept of Undue Hardship in Accommodations

In Canada, employers are legally required to accommodate employees with disabilities, including mental health conditions, up to the point of undue hardship. This means making adjustments such as flexible working hours, modified duties, or other accommodations to support the employee's mental health. However, when mental health conditions require ongoing accommodations, the boundary between reasonable accommodation and undue hardship can be difficult to define.

Undue hardship is typically reached when the accommodations required cause significant operational difficulties or expense. For example, if an employee's ongoing needs—such as frequent time off or adjustments to their responsibilities—start to impact the performance of the team or the financial sustainability of the business, employers may face challenging decisions.

It's important for employers to approach these situations with empathy, while also considering the needs of the team. Managers and Human Resources professionals should work together to create a plan that balances support for the individual with the broader needs of the organization. This includes being transparent with employees about the accommodations being made, and when adjustments might need to change.

Navigating Stigma and Creating Safe Conversations

One of the biggest challenges when managing mental health in the workplace is overcoming the stigma that surrounds it. There is often a reluctance to openly discuss the difficulties associated with managing complex mental health conditions, as these conversations can be perceived as insensitive. However, the inability to talk about these challenges can prevent the team from addressing the root causes of stress and frustration.

Managers can help reduce this stigma by fostering a culture where mental health is openly discussed and treated as a normal part of workplace dynamics. It's imperative that teams feel comfortable expressing their concerns in a way that is respectful and constructive, rather than allowing tensions to build. Open conversations, supported by ongoing training on mental health literacy, can ensure that all employees feel heard and valued, without creating divisions.

Balancing Empathy with Boundaries

Empathy is essential when supporting employees with mental health challenges, but it must be coupled with clear communication and boundaries to protect the well-being of everyone involved. Managers should work with their teams to set realistic expectations around what accommodations can be offered and ensure that the needs of the broader team are considered.

For example, a manager might set up regular check-ins with the employee to assess how accommodations are working and whether adjustments are needed. This open line of communication ensures that the employee feels supported while also allowing the manager to manage the team's workload effectively. By setting boundaries and maintaining transparency, managers can offer compassionate support without sacrificing their own well-being or the team's performance.

Managing mental health in the workplace, particularly when dealing with chronic or complex conditions, requires a thoughtful and inclusive approach. By recognizing the complexity of these conditions, fostering open communication, and balancing empathy with clear boundaries, employers can create a supportive environment that benefits both the individual and the broader team. This approach not only prevents burnout and resentment but also builds a healthier, more inclusive workplace culture.

CONCLUSION: NAVIGATING THE COMPLEXITIES OF MENTAL HEALTH IN THE WORKPLACE

Managing mental health in the workplace is a challenge that goes beyond providing time off, therapy options, or accommodations. While these elements are essential, they only address part of the equation. The real complexity lies in how mental health impacts not just the individual experiencing the condition but also the wider organization, including managers, coworkers, and overall workplace culture.

The narratives around mental health in the workplace often focus on the importance of providing support, which is undoubtedly critical. However, there is another side to the story that is rarely discussed—the emotional and operational toll that managing mental health conditions can take on everyone involved. For managers, especially those without adequate training or support, navigating an employee's chronic or complex mental health challenges can be exhausting and overwhelming. Balancing the needs of the individual with the demands of the team, all while trying to maintain productivity, requires a level of empathy and resilience that can quickly lead to burnout if not handled carefully.

Personality disorders and chronic mental health conditions add another layer of complexity. These conditions often manifest in behaviours that are challenging to manage in a workplace environment—whether it's emotional volatility, interpersonal conflicts, or fluctuating productivity. While employees living with these conditions deserve understanding and accommodations, it is equally important to recognize that managing these situations takes a significant toll on those around them. Colleagues may experience frustration or exhaustion from constantly adapting to an unpredictable dynamic, and managers may feel the weight of carrying both the individual's needs and the team's performance on their shoulders.

To navigate these complexities effectively, workplaces must adopt a multifaceted approach. One key component is fostering open, honest discussions about mental health—not just from the perspective of supporting the individual with the condition but also from the viewpoint of those who are managing and working alongside them. Creating space for these conversations helps to break down the stigma surrounding mental health and allows team members to express their challenges without fear of being seen as unsupportive or insensitive.

Empathy is, of course, essential in managing mental health in the workplace. Employees with mental health conditions need to feel that their workplace is a safe space where they can seek support without judgment. However, empathy must be balanced with clear boundaries. It's important that managers understand where to draw the line between supporting an employee's mental health needs and maintaining the overall health of the team. Setting realistic expectations, maintaining open communication, and establishing clear guidelines for accommodations can help managers create a balanced environment where everyone's needs are considered.

Another critical factor is the role of training and mental health literacy within organizations. Managers who are equipped with the tools and knowledge to recognize early signs of mental health struggles and respond effectively can make a significant difference in how these issues are handled. Moreover, ensuring that all employees are educated about mental health fosters a culture of understanding and support, reducing the stigma that often prevents people from speaking up about their struggles.

The legal framework in Canada requires employers to accommodate employees with disabilities, including mental health conditions, to the point of undue hardship. However, understanding what constitutes undue hardship can be tricky when dealing with mental health, particularly in cases where behaviour becomes disruptive to the broader team. By having clear policies and action plans in place, organizations can better navigate this balance, ensuring they meet their legal and ethical obligations without compromising the well-being of the team or the organization's ability to function.

Ultimately, the goal of managing mental health in the workplace should be to create an environment where both individuals with mental health conditions and their colleagues feel supported. This means acknowledging that mental health is not a one-size-fits-all issue. Every situation is unique and requires thoughtful, tailored solutions that balance empathy with the practical realities of the workplace.

By fostering open discussions about the realities of managing complex mental health cases and creating a balance between support and boundaries, organizations can navigate these challenges in a way that respects both the individual's needs and the limits of what can reasonably be managed. It is through this nuanced approach that workplaces can move beyond simplistic narratives and create truly inclusive environments that promote mental well-being for all employees.

ABOUT THE AUTHOR

I'm Frederique Bergeron, an Human Resources leader and author with over 25 years of experience helping organizations build supportive, inclusive, and mentally healthy workplaces. I'm passionate about creating environments where people can thrive, and I've dedicated my career to developing strategies that prioritize employee well-being, mental health, and organizational resilience. Through my work in talent management and organizational development, I've guided businesses through the complexities of accommodating mental health challenges while maintaining strong, high-performance cultures.

In my latest book, **The Silent Struggle: Navigating Mental Health Challenges in the Workplace**, I explore the often-overlooked impact of mental health on both individuals and teams. With real-world case studies and practical advice, I aim to help managers and leaders balance empathy with the operational realities of running a business. Mental health is complex, and I believe that by addressing it openly, we can create healthier, more productive workplaces for everyone.

As an advocate for mental health awareness, I believe that open dialogue, flexible policies, and ongoing support systems are essential to fostering workplaces where everyone feels valued and understood. Through my writing, I provide the tools leaders need to build mentally healthy organizations where both businesses and employees can thrive.

www.ingramcontent.com/pod-product-compliance
Lightning Source LLC
Chambersburg PA
CBHW070951220526
45471CB00007B/2987